DISC 17

DISC Behavioral Model
Self-Assessment

Perception → Orientation → Behavior

CPLE INTERNATIONAL | Center for Police Leadership & Ethics

www.cpleinternational.org

Copyright © 2021 by Glocal Press

All rights reserved

ISBN 978-0-9817116-6-9

No part of this publication may be reproduced, stored in a retrieval system, or transmitted, in any form or by any means, electronic, mechanical, photocopying, recording, or otherwise, without the prior written permission of the author, except as permitted under the 1976 United States Copyright Act.

This publication is sold with the understanding that neither the publisher nor the author is engaged in rendering legal or professional services. If legal or policy advice is prudent, the reader should seek competent assistance. in that area.

For bulk sales of the *DISC 17 Self-Assessment* or to inquire about attending or hosting a CPLE DISC course, please contact info@cpleinternational.org.

Center for Police Leadership & Ethics International

www.cpleinternational.org

About our DISC Behavioral Assessment (*DISC 17*)

DISC 17 comprises 24 groups of descriptors. The groups are arranged in a forced-choice format with four words in each group. This format forces you to choose a *most* and *least* descriptor in each of the 24 groupings. You may find none of the words in a column describe you or perhaps more than one word in each column accurately describes you. To the extent possible, choose the most and least accurate recognizing the *most* descriptor may not always describe you perfectly, and similarly, the *least* descriptor does not mean you never display that characteristic.

The ipsative or forced-choice format was used because it is arguably the best method to gain accurate data and results in assessments such as this. It is simple, consistent, and more easily compared to other participant's assessments. It eliminates the *don't know*, *neutral*, and *not applicable* responses found in many other surveys. Participants must commit to an answer. Perhaps, the most important benefit of this formatting is the mitigation of bias such as social desirability or response bias.

A Few Thoughts Before You Begin

DISC 17 is not a test. There are no right or wrong responses just as there are no right or wrong results. Be honest with yourself when choosing your responses. It is very easy to answer the responses from the mindset of *Who I Want to Be*. For the instrument to be accurate, push through that natural desire and respond from a view of *Who I Really Am*.

Attempt taking the assessment with a broad lens - what are your preferences in general. However, you may need to put yourself in a specific context when responding – home, work, church, sports, etc. Adding a contextual framework may help you decide between two responses if you find yourself having difficulty narrowing the choices from four to one. The instrument, however, is designed to accommodate this very issue. The first time I took the assessment, I commented to my colleague, "There were several questions that could have gone either way between two of the words." He said, "Ok, take it again with you answering those questions with the other word." Both times I came out the same specific pattern.

Context plays one more significant role. Words mean different things in different settings. Consider the word *talkative*. An extrovert who is all about people and engagement obviously would identify with this word. Yet, a person who detests large crowds and public speaking also may identify with this word if they are talkative in their small work groups or with family. Again, placing yourself in a specific context at least will offer consistency in your focus.

Some of you may feel conflicted taking the assessment. "I feel like I am contradicting myself with some of these answers." Don't let that bother you. Most of us feel that way, and 99% of the time it does not affect the outcomes of the assessment. 1% of assessments have responses that contradict other responses so much that they cancel each other out. We will talk about that later, but do not fret over that extremely low possibility. Just be honest with yourself on each of the 24 questions.

Finally, consider not spending too much time on each question. Give each question its due diligence, but research over the years generally shows results are more accurate when respondents go with their first choice as opposed to overanalyzing it.

Let's Get Started

DISC 17 comprises 24 groups of descriptors. The groups are arranged in a forced-choice format with four words in each group. On the following page (page 3), place **ONE** check mark or X in the **MOST** column to describe which word best describes you. Place **ONE** check mark or X in the **LEAST** column to describe which word least describes you.

Example:

	MOST	LEAST
Eager	X	
Brave		
Rules-oriented		
Tactful		X

©2021 Reproduction of this instrument is prohibited

Response Page 1

Choose <u>one</u> Most and <u>one</u> Least in each of the 24 groups of words.

1. Eager
   Brave
   Rules
   Tactful

2. Gregarious
   Precise
   Opinionated
   Calm

3. Systematic
   Charismatic
   Domineering
   Sympathetic

4. Inspiring
   Decisive
   Conforming
   Detailed

5. Steady
   Bold
   Spontaneous
   Exact

6. Captivating
   Cooperative
   Determined
   Compliant

7. Aggressive
   Convincing
   Kind
   Specific

8. Enthusiastic
   Methodical
   Assertive
   Tolerant

9. Obliging
   Stimulating
   Guarded
   Outspoken

10. Neutral
    Impulsive
    Predictable
    Powerful

11. Fun-loving
    Loyal
    Imposing
    Organized

12. Controlling
    Withdrawn
    Sincere
    Unplanned

13. Iron-willed
    Structured
    Animated
    Neighborly

14. Eloquent
    Perfectionist
    Courageous
    Passive

15. Extrovert
    Direct
    Inflexible
    Content

16. Factual
    Helpful
    Magnetic
    Urgent

17. Jovial
    Detailed
    Audacious
    Soft-spoken

18. Cheerful
    Risk-taker
    Talkative
    Prepared

19. Careful
    Candid
    Persuasive
    Sincere

20. Caring
    Logical
    Exciting
    Daring

21. Popular
    Submissive
    Fearless
    Disciplined

22. Sensitive
    Vibrant
    Orderly
    Impatient

23. Visionary
    Passive
    Thorough
    Overbearing

24. Easygoing
    Outgoing
    Stubborn
    Forceful

©2021 Reproduction of this instrument is prohibited

On the next page, circle the letter under the **Most** column and the **Least** column in each grouping that corresponds to your responses on the response page.

Example

Response

	MOST	LEAST
Eager	X	
Brave		
Rule-oriented		
Tactful		X

Response Analysis Page

	MOST	LEAST
Eager	(I)	I
Brave	D	D
Rule-oriented	S	S
Tactful	C	(C)

©2021 Reproduction of this instrument is prohibited

Response Analysis Page

		M	L
1.	Eager	I	I
	Brave	D	D
	Rules	C	C
	Tactful	S	S

		M	L
7.	Aggressive	D	D
	Convincing	I	I
	Kind	S	S
	Specific	C	C

		M	L
13.	Iron-willed	D	D
	Structured	C	C
	Animated	I	I
	Neighborly	S	S

		M	L
19.	Careful	C	C
	Candid	D	D
	Persuasive	I	I
	Sincere	S	S

		M	L
2.	Gregarious	I	I
	Precise	C	C
	Opinionated	D	D
	Calm	S	S

		M	L
8.	Enthusiastic	I	I
	Methodical	C	C
	Assertive	D	D
	Tolerant	S	S

		M	L
14.	Eloquent	I	I
	Perfectionist	C	C
	Courageous	D	D
	Passive	S	S

		M	L
20.	Caring	S	S
	Logical	C	C
	Exciting	I	I
	Daring	D	D

		M	L
3.	Systematic	C	C
	Charismatic	I	I
	Domineering	D	D
	Sympathetic	S	S

		M	L
9.	Obliging	S	S
	Stimulating	I	I
	Guarded	C	C
	Outspoken	D	D

		M	L
15.	Extrovert	I	I
	Direct	D	D
	Inflexible	C	C
	Content	S	S

		M	L
21.	Popular	I	I
	Submissive	S	S
	Fearless	D	D
	Disciplined	C	C

		M	L
4.	Inspiring	I	I
	Decisive	D	D
	Conforming	S	S
	Detailed	C	C

		M	L
10.	Neutral	S	S
	Impulsive	I	I
	Predictable	C	C
	Powerful	D	D

		M	L
16.	Factual	C	C
	Helpful	S	S
	Magnetic	I	I
	Urgent	D	D

		M	L
22.	Sensitive	S	S
	Vibrant	I	I
	Orderly	C	C
	Impatient	D	D

		M	L
5.	Steady	S	S
	Bold	D	D
	Spontaneous	I	I
	Exact	C	C

		M	L
11.	Fun-loving	I	I
	Loyal	S	S
	Imposing	D	D
	Organized	C	C

		M	L
17.	Jovial	I	I
	Detailed	C	C
	Audacious	D	D
	Soft-spoken	S	S

		M	L
23.	Visionary	I	I
	Passive	S	S
	Thorough	C	C
	Overbearing	D	D

		M	L
6.	Captivating	I	I
	Cooperative	S	S
	Determined	D	D
	Compliant	C	C

		M	L
12.	Controlling	D	D
	Withdrawn	C	C
	Sincere	S	S
	Unplanned	I	I

		M	L
18.	Cheerful	S	S
	Risk-taker	D	D
	Talkative	I	I
	Prepared	C	C

		M	L
24.	Easygoing	S	S
	Outgoing	I	I
	Stubborn	C	C
	Forceful	D	D

©2021 Reproduction of this instrument is prohibited

Response Analysis Instructions Continued...

2. Record the following numbers under **Your Numbers**. Count all the **D**s you circled in the **Most** columns in all 24 responses. Write that number in the Most column on the **D** row. Count all the **I**s you circled in the Most columns in all 24 responses. Write that number in the Most column on the **I** row. Continue this with the **S**s and **C**s. When the Most column is complete, continue the same process with the **Least** column.

3. Using the **D** row, subtract the **Least** column number from the **Most** column number and write that number in the **Results** row (Most – Least = Least). Then repeat this process for the I, S, and C rows. *Note: You will have negative numbers in your Results.*

Sample

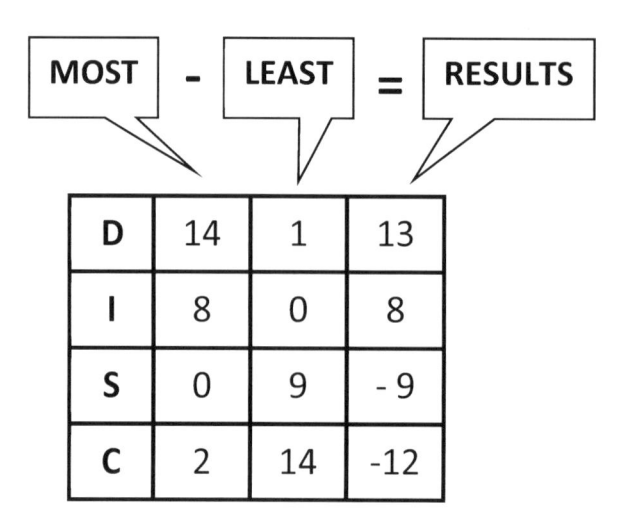

MOST − LEAST = RESULTS

	MOST	LEAST	RESULTS
D	14	1	13
I	8	0	8
S	0	9	-9
C	2	14	-12

Your Numbers

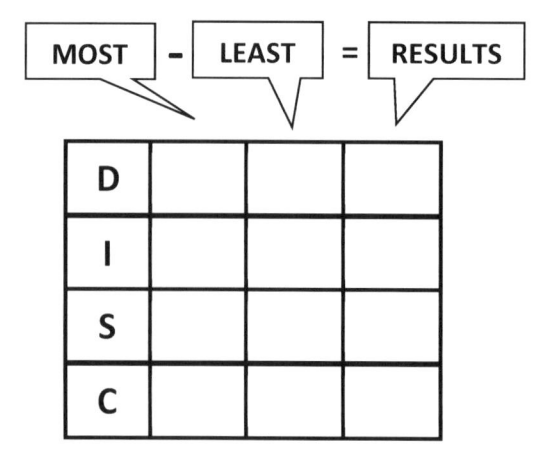

MOST − LEAST = RESULTS

	MOST	LEAST	RESULTS
D			
I			
S			
C			

©2021 Reproduction of this instrument is prohibited

4. Using the numbers from the ***RESULTS*** column, circle the corresponding numbers for D, I, S, and C on **Your Graph**.

5. Connect the circles on the graph from left to right with straight lines.

- Please see the sample graph based on the preceding numbers. You will notice in the participant's highest dimension is D with the second highest dimension being I. We would categorize this person's DISC profile as a D/I. The nuances in the high and lows of these two dimensions above the bold horizontal line, as well as the two below the line, matter. But the D/I designation is a good place to start in identifying this participant's natural perceptions and responses to the world.

Sample

D	I	S	C
19	19	19	19
17	17	17	17
15	15	15	15
13	13	13	13
11	11	11	11
9	9	9	9
7	7	7	7
5	5	5	5
3	3	3	3
1	1	1	1
-1	-1	-1	-1
-3	-3	-3	-3
-5	-5	-5	-5
-7	-7	-7	-7
-9	-9	-9	-9
-11	-11	-11	-11
-13	-13	-13	-13
-15	-15	-15	-15
-17	-17	-17	-17
-19	-19	-19	-19

©2021 Reproduction of this instrument is prohibited

Your Graph

D	I	S	C
19	19	19	19
17	17	17	17
15	15	15	15
13	13	13	13
11	11	11	11
9	9	9	9
7	7	7	7
5	5	5	5
3	3	3	3
1	1	1	1
-1	-1	-1	-1
-3	-3	-3	-3
-5	-5	-5	-5
-7	-7	-7	-7
-9	-9	-9	-9
-11	-11	-11	-11
-13	-13	-13	-13
-15	-15	-15	-15
-17	-17	-17	-17
-19	-19	-19	-19

6. Find a Reasonable Facsimile of Your Graph on the following pages and circle the Quadrant number found in the angle of the Quadrant. As there are infinite numbers of specific profiles, and DISC is just as much about your dimensions below the line as it is your dimensions above the line, it is not practical or necessary to be exact.

- A small percentage of people have profiles with a single dimension above the line and three below (about 5%). We depicted those graphs using Quadrants 1 through 4. Most of us (about 80%) have two DISC dimensions above the line and two below the line, which are depicted with Quadrants 5 through 12. Roughly 15% of profiles have three dimensions above the line and one below. The DBA also uses Quadrants 5 through 12 to handle these profiles without calling them out specifically. Of the people with two above and two below, two combinations are rare enough many instruments pay little to no attention to them - the I and C combination (I/C or C/I) and the D and S combination (D/S or S/D). Because they are just as significant as the other more common or classic profiles, *DISC 17* gives them their own unique narratives. These profiles are represented by quadrants 13 through 16. The final profile depicted in this text is shown in Quadrant 17 – the tight or compressed pattern.

©2021 Reproduction of this instrument is prohibited

Refer to this diagram if your graph has <u>one dimension above</u> the horizontal line and <u>three below</u>.

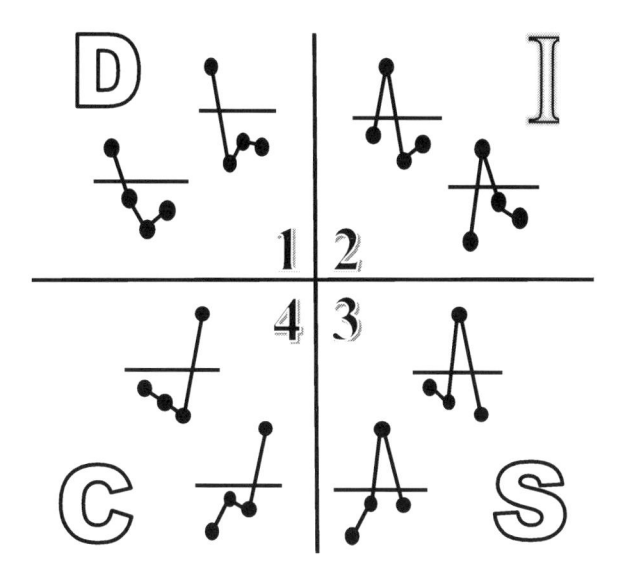

Using the number located in the Quadrant angle (1-4), find the corresponding page with your narrative description. Read the narrative and see how accurately it describes you.

Refer to the following diagram if your graph has <u>two dimensions above</u> the line and <u>two below</u>. (If your top two dimensions are S & D or I & C, move to the next page)

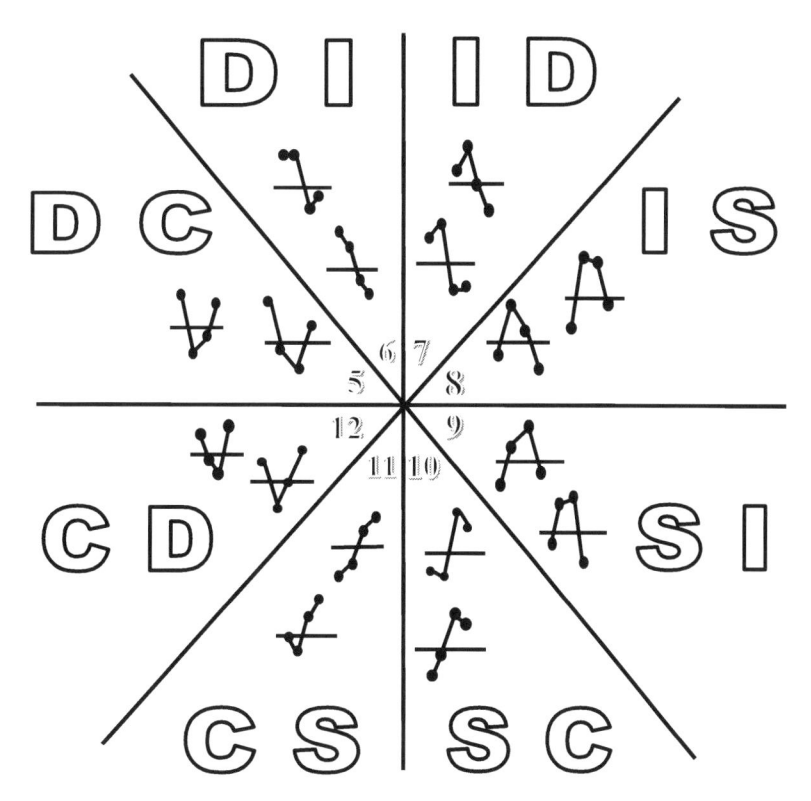

Using the number located in the Quadrant angle (5-12), find the corresponding page with your narrative description. Read the narrative and see how accurately it describes you.

©2021 Reproduction of this instrument is prohibited

A Few Uncommon but Just as Important Graphs

Diagonal Combinations

Most two-dimension combinations follow the axis in a clock-wise or counter clock-wise manner. For example, common two-dimension combinations are D/I, I/S, S/C, and C/D (or the reverse…I/D, D/C, C/S, and S/I). However, a small percentage of the population crosses the axis diagonally (D/S or S/D and C/I or I/C). Some estimates are as small as ½ of 1% for the D/S and S/D combinations and 3% for the C/I and I/C combinations). Unlike many other DISC instruments, we have found through decades of research and teaching that these graphs are better explained on their own rather than being absorbed in more umbrella patterns. If your graph is more like these, please read your narrative on the corresponding page (Quadrants 13-16).

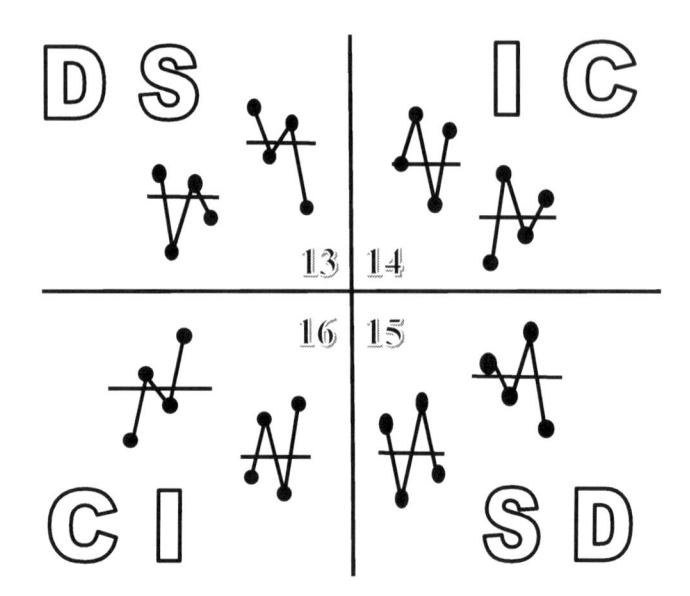

Flatliners ☺
Narrative # 17

The last graph deserving its own explanation is the *Tight* or *Compressed* Pattern or what I more fondly call, *Flatliners*. No, we are not talking about people who have no personality! These are graphs in which all four dimensions are close to the horizontal line. A few examples are below. Please read narrative #17 if all four of your dimensions hover close to the line.

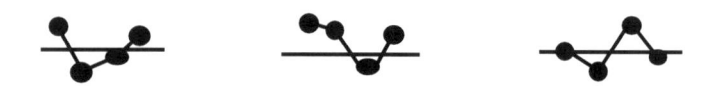

©2021 Reproduction of this instrument is prohibited

Over and Unders

Sometimes participants will present four above the line or four below the line as shown in the examples below:

The reality is these patterns do not really exist. When participants choose an adjective that is weighted for a particular dimension, this prevents them from choosing an adjective weighted for one of the other three dimensions. This means it is impossible to get a high score on all four traits and impossible to get a low score on all four traits.

Math is usually the culprit. If you have four above or below the line, take a few minutes to recount your responses and make sure you correctly subtracted the Least column from the Most column to get the answer for the Results column (A column – B column = C column). Remember, you will have negative numbers in the Results column. If the math is correct, retake the assessment with a clearer focus on a specific context or role (e.g. work, home, school, church).

Notes Page

DISC 17

Behavioral Profile
Narratives

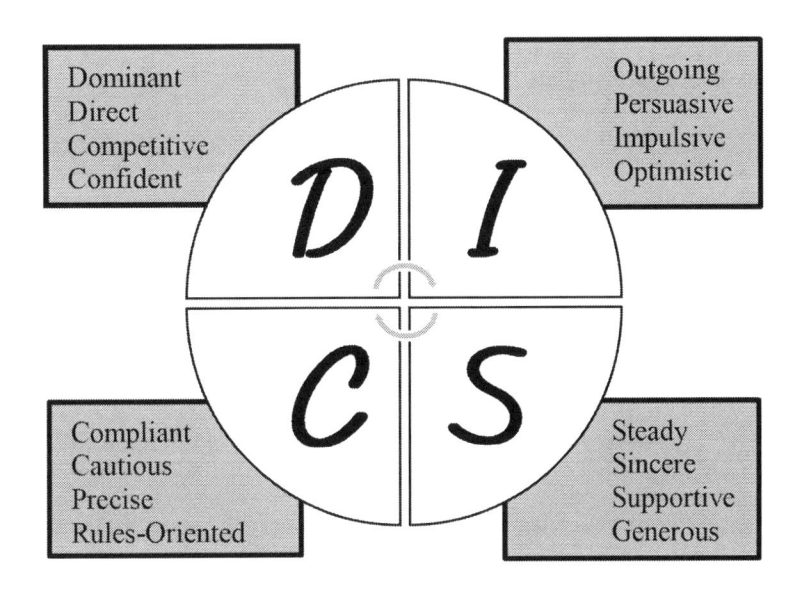

D — Dominant, Direct, Competitive, Confident	**I** — Outgoing, Persuasive, Impulsive, Optimistic
C — Compliant, Cautious, Precise, Rules-Oriented	**S** — Steady, Sincere, Supportive, Generous

The following narratives represent the 17 DISC profiles found in the preceding graphs. While we will explore the model in much more detail as the text progresses, each narrative concludes with brief suggestions moving forward as you begin to learn more about yourself and others. Categorizing complex human behavioral preferences into only 17 categories is obviously fraught with generalizations. The nuances and degrees with which your highs and lows fall on the graph are infinite. And remember, the instrument measures your natural response to the world not your complete personality. For these reasons, rarely will any single narrative completely describe you. We are looking for patterns of behavior. I think you will find a more than adequate level of specificity and accuracy with your profile narrative – more than enough to equip you with a much deeper understanding of both your natural responses to the world as well as those of others.

The High D

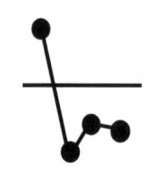

Quadrant 1

The High *D* profile represents *Dominance*. Perhaps more than anything, you value control. Whether you are ready to admit this or not, you generally view your environment as less than desirable, and you almost always view yourself as more powerful than your environment. With this convergence arises a person with a strong sense of independence and personal accountability. Because you thrive on autonomy, you are easily demoralized in a restrictive environment. You may be so self-reliant that you often gravitate towards *going it alone* in many aspects of your life. You've probably said to yourself on many occasions, "I know it will get done the way I want it if I do it myself." Control does not mean you are always barking orders although commanding others to do your bidding is well within your comfort zone. Control to you may mean sitting back and watching quietly knowing you are in control or contemplating ways to gain control should the need arise.

You also value reach. It is not enough to control your immediate circumstances. You have a strong drive to grow your circumstances, to expand your influence. Sometimes your quest for greater reach manifests in strong ambition for rank and positions of authority. Sometimes it is more about informal power and influence.

You are about results, and you bore easily. This can make life very interesting. You are much more concerned with getting the job done and moving on to the next project as opposed to getting the job done right. This is not to say you do not value a good product or want to make good decisions; the product or decision just does not have to be perfect. You would rather get ten things done at an A- today as opposed to one thing at an A+.

You are strong-willed, independent, mission-focused, and rarely satisfied. This drives your penchant for innovation and hard work. You attack life never waiting for things to happen. You are a doer. You not only compete with others but continuously compete with yourself. You clearly identify with the quote made by one of the greatest tennis players of our time (and high D), Martina Navratilova. "Whoever said, 'it's not whether you win or lose that counts,' probably lost."

You believe in creating your own luck and success. As such, you thrive in new and uncharted territories and can be counted on as an innovative and dynamic force in whatever context you find yourself. You are a problem solver. Not one to mince words or avoid conflict, you are direct and clear with your communications. You thrive under stress and tight deadlines. You are decisive and comfortable with high degrees of risk when making decisions.

The growth areas of this profile also are prevalent. Because you can be so self-reliant, you may not rely on the wisdom of others to influence your decision making. Indeed, you often need to experience failure even when others have counseled, warned, or begged you to make a different decision. You can be very judgmental – judgments often rooted in what you see of value as opposed to what others or the organization view as important. Patience is not your virtue and for good reason. You detest procrastination and avoidance of work. You despise it in yourself and others, and you do not tolerate incompetence. While failure may be your deepest fear, your quickest trigger to anger is being taken advantage of – your perception is all that matters. This results-oriented, impatient style often projects a "my way or the highway" persona, which may lead to communication and conflict challenges as people may see you as too domineering, abrasive, unempathetic, and even obnoxious at times.

Moving Forward: Of all your strengths, as with the High I, S, and C profiles, balance may be your single most important growth opportunity. Any strength overused may become a liability. Developing balance in your behavior requires changes in your perceptions of the world around you. Recognize that not all contexts are hostile or unfriendly. Tone down the need for control in every aspect of your life. It is okay to be a follower from time to time.

Your desire for control coupled with a results-orientated mindset may affect your capacity to delegate. Some high D profiles are weak in this area choosing to do most things themselves. However, the savvy high D knows the best and quickest results are usually accomplished through teams making this person an exceptional delegator. The savvy high Ds take the time to teach and coach. They empower their followers to make decisions. Yet, even with the practical high Ds, they still do not tolerate incompetence, procrastination, or perceived inadequacies of any kind. Impatience and even a strong temper often result. Micromanaging in your delegation may be a problem. Work on your delegation skills if this is a growth area for you.

You view rules as guidelines or suggestions (unless they are your rules). This is exactly the type of behavior that gets things done and probably in unique and ambitious ways. However, rules are usually in place for a reason. Disregarding them at leisure will ultimately lead to failure and certainly alienate those around you who like following rules.

You need to stay busy always moving and doing something. You may even judge your self-worth on what you get accomplished today. Under pressure, you usually rid yourself of stress through ranting and challenging others. Conflict seems to calm your inner self. In a fight or flight scenario, you almost always fight. As a result, other profiles may feel intimidated or unnecessarily controlled. Consider taking time to relax a little even during stressful times. It will help you as well as those around you.

Recognize the need for others, the value of teams and alliances, in accomplishing great things. Remember what Vince Lombardi offered. "Individual commitment to a group effort: That is what makes a team work, a company work, a society work, a civilization work." Work on displaying a sense of caring for others. I am not suggesting to a High D that you need to suddenly become warm and fuzzy. I am only observing that people need to know others care about them, particularly if you are in a leadership role. Asking questions and actively listening will help demonstrate how much you value the people around you. Be careful in your communications, particularly with high S profiles. You may come across as pushy, aggressive, and overpowering. Each of us needs to behave in all four DISC dimensions throughout the day depending on the needs of the situation. Work on recognizing when and how to elevate the power of the other three dimensions when the people or situation around you dictate.

The High *I*

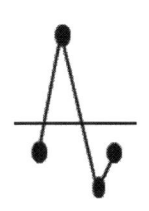

Quadrant 2

The High *I* profile represents *Influence*. You almost always view your surroundings as friendly and yourself in control. Your control is informed through exceptional communication skills. With D, S, and C dimensions below the line, you are all about people. Whether in small groups or the largest of crowds, you thrive in contexts where you can engage with others, where you are able to express your thoughts, ideas, and opinions.

But expression is not enough. You want (need) to pull people towards your vision. And you have plenty of vision. Of all four umbrella dimensions, you are the most visionary always looking to the future in exciting and inspiring ways. Whether in personal relationships, work environment, or most settings you find yourself in, you are the one with the positive attitude, persuasive capabilities, enthusiasm, and confidence moving the conversation and people forward.

Because of your people orientation, you place a significant emphasis on building relationships. In the work setting, you are all about networking within and outside the organization. You know your kid's teachers by first name. At home, you know all the neighbors, and they all know you. After all, you are fun to be around because you carry conversations in otherwise awkward settings. You entertain people with your quick wit, humor, and charm. Your enthusiasm for life and all things possible is contagious. You inspire people. And you make people feel good about themselves. You also tend to show more tolerance across many areas of humanity from behavior and insights to demographics such as religion, race, and cultural differences. Your zest for life is powerful. It is almost palpable in the eyes of those around you. You are an idea person always challenging yourself and others with new and exciting possibilities for the future.

Just as the other profiles with one dimension above the line, you also have areas that could stand some improvement. Prestige and status are of high value to you. What people around you may not know is that your motives can be ego driven, and manipulation your tool of persuasion. You don't just want people to believe in what you are selling because it is a great idea or product. You want them to believe in you. Your ego requires it, and public humiliation, lack of inclusion, and loss of social acceptance may be your greatest fears. Your emotions are a powerful tool in winning friends and building relationships, but they often emerge unrestrained and even animated. Your focus on people means you have less focus on things. Planning, organization, and details are not your friends. This convergence often means you still value success and attaining goals, but the excitement of the idea and the journey you take with others are much more important to you than the goal itself.

Moving Forward: As with the High D, S, and C profiles, balance may be your single most important growth opportunity. Remember, any strength overused may become a liability. Spontaneity is a good example. Your inclination for impulsive behavior can be inspiring and exciting but overused, it can lead down a path of disorganization and procrastination. Your playfulness is entertaining and lightens otherwise heavy or boring situations, but timing is everything. Some high I profiles have difficulty knowing the difference between fun time and game time. Similarly, in your efforts to inspire and make people feel good about themselves, you can overuse praise. Praise is a wonderful thing but use it accurately and judiciously, or it will lose its power and may make you appear insincere and superficial. Developing balance in your behavior requires changes in your perceptions of the world around you. Recognize there are times where your strength of personality will not carry the day. This acceptance may help you better prepare for tasks instead of relying on your charm, quick intellect, and *gift of gab*.

Larger-than-life personalities like you can sometimes use people for their own ends. If you recognize yourself doing this, try viewing those around you not as means to an end but as the end themselves.

Give some thought to overextending yourself. Because of your deep optimism, need for constant challenge, and desire to make people happy, you tend to overcommit beyond either your capabilities or time constraints. Time management is often a challenge for you.

You love being around people, and you are a talker. Work on your listening skills if this is a growth area for you. It will empower others around and better ingratiate them to your cause. Consider giving others the center of attention allowing them to freely express themselves without interruption. You need the energy and social acceptance provided by expressing yourself, but occasionally, it is okay to be quiet (and as my wife will say, "Give others a break!"). Each of us needs to behave in all four DISC dimensions throughout the day depending on the needs of the situation. Work on recognizing when and how to elevate the power of the other three dimensions when the people or situation around you dictate.

The High S

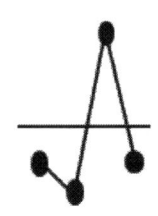

Quadrant 3

The High S profile represents *steadiness* and *sincerity*. You almost always view your surroundings as positive but often feel less powerful than those surroundings. This may be one of the reasons you display such a high level of respect for others.

You are dependable, considerate, and generous. You love helping others. You are a team player embracing collaboration and cooperation. In fact, just as your High I friends, you need the social acceptance of your friends and coworkers. And just as you give sincere praise to others, you want that from them.

Many consider you shy and introverted. However, this really depends on the situation. In small, comfortable groups of friends and coworkers, you are very outgoing, very chatty at times. But in large settings, you may become very quiet, often clinging to a friend or loved one for security. You are not scared in these settings, just a little apprehensive and uncomfortable.

You are everyone's friend because of your sincere, supportive, and caring attitude. You care more about others than yourself, so you tend to be a great listener. You have a sense of modesty about you that endears you quickly to others. With no hidden agenda and such a deep-rooted genuineness, people feel comfortable and non-threatened in your presence. People trust you.

But you still have growth opportunities ahead of you just as your high D, I, and C friends. High S profiles can be possessive at times. This occasionally manifests with things if you view that object as a source of security (e.g. the proverbial child's blankie). More often, the possessiveness presents with people. You prefer smaller, informal groups so friendships mean a lot to you. You may become resentful if you perceive others intruding on those relationships or if close friends start paying more attention to others. The possessive nature of the high S seems to lessen with age and wisdom but be careful of this snare even into your older years.

Your sense of loyalty is admirably strong, but it may overshadow the flaws, misjudgments, and poor decisions of those around you. This strong loyalty, almost blind at times, coupled with an innate aversion to conflict and confrontation presents a dynamic where you may avoid holding people accountable.

You are a patient, steady, and calming voice throughout the day. Yet, crisis can change this very quickly. You tend to be resistant to change and need time to adapt to new and dynamic environments. High D and C profiles see life in clear black and white contrasts. You view life more as a gray area often seeing the benefits of both sides of an issue. While this optimistic and objective lens can be beneficial, it also may lead to indecision and over accommodation. Most of the time, you are happy and content – another reason everyone loves high Ss. The challenge is that contentment leads to a proclivity for status quo. Thus, innovation and risk-taking are not characteristics you embrace easily.

Moving Forward: As with the High D, I, and C profiles, balance may be your single most important growth opportunity. Because you view your surroundings as more powerful, you typically do not embrace conflict unless your back is against the wall - peace and harmony are your comfort zones. This may appear to those around you as submission, weakness, or insecurity, which can lead to being taking advantage of or ineffectiveness in your leadership roles. Work on your confidence. Train yourself to feel strong and empowered in otherwise seeming environments.

Work on your conflict skills, particularly in your leadership roles (supervisor, parent, coach). You are a kind and sincere person, so you are generally very adept at brokering peace. But remember, leaders do not avoid conflict or try to crush it. There are times you need to embrace conflict in a constructive manner. Managing healthy conflict is good for your tribe (home, work, teams) and good for you as an individual.

Because you do not want to hurt people's feelings or *be the bad guy*, you tend to be more indirect in your communications often taking a softer approach to difficult conversations. Certainly, there is a time and place for tact and a more lenient approach but work on being clearer and more direct in your communications, particularly when you are in a leadership position.

Because you are all about people, you spend less time focused on things. Avoid procrastination. Learn to balance the people and things in your life. And yes, your humility ingratiates you with everyone. But remember there are times when the people around you want, even need, to see confidence and decisiveness in your approach. Each of us needs to behave in all four DISC dimensions throughout the day depending on the needs of the situation. Work on recognizing when and how to elevate the power of the other three dimensions when the people or situation around you dictate.

The High C

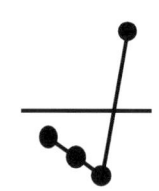

Quadrant 4

With D, I, and S dimensions below the line, the High *C* profile represents *compliance* above all. You like to follow the rules. Rules give you a sense of security, control, predictability, and organization amidst the chaos of the world. As your gravitation towards conformity extends to people, you rarely challenge authority unless those in power are violating the rules, policies, or accepted social norms. Usually reserved and not prone to confrontation, you can become a fierce fighter in these situations.

You are a critical thinker strongly valuing accuracy, details, and facts. You need to understand the way things work at what some would consider a micro level. Because of your analytical nature and need to get things right, you place great emphasis on meticulous planning. You have often echoed the old saying, "If it's worth doing, it's worth doing right."

You are self-disciplined and deliberate in thought and deed. You are focused. You have the ability to block out distractions better than most people. When immersed in a project, you may not even hear those around you talking or the TV or the phone ring or even a siren outside. You are a hard worker. You are no quitter. In fact, you can be absolutely dogged in your quest to learn, build, and lead.

You are precise in your actions and words and expect the same of others. While DISC does not measure values, beliefs, and character, you do tend to be honest because otherwise would be breaking societal rules and expectations. People who exaggerate, lie, and even use large generalizations in their speech highly frustrate you.

In fact, people in general often frustrate you. You may even consider yourself socially awkward often avoiding social interaction. You certainly value family and close friendships, but most of the time you are completely comfortable alone. Indeed, too much interaction with people drains you of energy – the classic introvert.

Because you highly value correctness, you need time to complete your tasks. Short deadlines and last-minute challenges are strong demotivators for you. You want perfection and nothing perfect happens without the time to plan and analyze every consideration and consequence. You are normally reserved in your emotions letting the facts speak for themselves. However, you can become irate, even insubordinate, when what you perceive as unrealistic expectations and time restraints are thrust upon you.

You can be shy and subdued, particularly in environments you view as unfriendly. The environment does not have to be hostile as in shots fired or the building burning down. It may be something as seemingly innocuous as being at your spouse's work party, which you have been dreading for weeks. It could be you have not had much sleep lately, so you will perceive no environment as friendly. It simply could be the weather. Rainy Monday mornings generally do not put many people in good moods.

Moving Forward: As with the High D, I, and S profiles, balance may be your single most important growth opportunity. Strong critical thinking skills help define your lens of the world and subsequent response to it. But any skill overused may become a liability. Your need to critically analyze every aspect of a decision may lead to what is referred to as *analysis paralysis,* which can create a situation where you get so bogged down in the scrutiny of the issues the decision never gets made. Jeff Boss suggested several considerations to improve in this area. Set a drop-dead time for your projects and decisions. Recognize that the moons will never align exactly – perfection does not always have to be the end goal. Curb your inclination to dig deeper into every aspect of the situation, follow every new detail that arises, and explore every hypothetical consequence. Establishing parameters for what you truly need to know as opposed to what you would like to know will help mitigate what appears to many as procrastination or indecision.

Because you generally view your surroundings as unfriendly, you sometimes portray a sense of pessimism. Most people want to buy into a bright future. They want to be around those who inspire them with their optimism and enthusiasm. The last thing anyone wants to hear when they have a great idea is, "It won't work because…." If this is a growth area for you, consider framing your perspective and response something like, "Your idea may be difficult for a variety of reasons, but no great accomplishments were ever easy. Let's think this through together how to overcome some apparent obstacles as we forward." With this altered view, you still retain the skepticism of your inner wiring but offer a path forward if that person is willing to work hard and meet reality head-on.

Given your propensity towards things as opposed to people, give some thought to your communication and conflict skills. You win most arguments on merit because you almost always know the policies and stats better than your opponent. But winning is a subjective concept. High Ds care little for rules and facts. Unless they made the rules, they quite often look at them as barriers to accomplishing what needs to be done. High I's value the argument itself because it a time for them to engage and persuade others to their cause. They may value intangibles (vision, dreams, ideals) much more than your facts and even win others to their cause because of their contagious rhetoric. You could win the battle but lose the war. Give some consideration to the notion that other personalities may not connect with your position just because facts and figures are on your side. Each of us needs to behave in all four DISC dimensions throughout the day depending on the needs of the situation. Work on recognizing when and how to elevate the power of the other three dimensions when the people or situation around you dictate.

The D/C

Quadrant 5

The *D/C* combination represents D and C dimensions above the line with S and I below the line. We all are a blend of all four dimensions, but the D/C profile behaves primarily with D tendencies and secondarily with C tendencies. Fluctuating between the two dimensions may appear seamless or abrupt at times. You often act neither as a pure D nor pure C due to the thorough blending of the two dimensions (and the two below the line) creating a profile that is unique in itself.

You are persistent and results-driven. The D in you is active, almost aggressive in your approach to life. The C is about perfection, accuracy, and intellectual curiosity. You may best be characterized as someone who wants things done your way, and they need to be done right.

You are self-disciplined, deliberate, and focused. You can block out distractions better than most people. When immersed in a project, you may not even hear those around you talking or the TV or the phone ring or even a siren outside. You are a hard worker. You are no quitter. In fact, you can be absolutely dogged in your quest to learn, build, and lead.

Often the loner, you seldom seek advice from other people. When you do, you ask sharp questions even if unpopular. You prefer to learn and create through trial and error, or you study alone. You will work with others, particularly as you have matured over the years, but you still would rather work alone. You frustrate easily when you have to wait on others to do their part, and frankly, you do not like to share control. You are highly critical of both yourself and others with a tendency to correct people when they make mistakes, even to the point of highlighting errors they may view as minor and inconsequential. Your bluntness is sometimes perceived as fresh and honest with no hidden agenda and sometimes perceived as insensitive, condescending, and even self-righteous. You can be skeptical of people's motives and sometimes prefer not to share information unless absolutely necessary. When communication with others is essential, you tend to be clear and concise, focusing on practical issues and tasks.

You sometimes struggle with delegation when in a leadership role although you clearly recognize its value. There is not enough time in the day for you to do everything you want to get accomplished. You know delegation is the only path. Yet, your propensity to *go it alone* can get in the way. When you do delegate, you can be clear in your communication and precise with the instructions. Yet, you also can micromanage and become very critical when things do not progress in the time or way you deem appropriate. You believe in getting things done right and rarely are afraid to state your position vigorously and directly.

Willpower abounds in your approach to tasks. You are dogged determined and have strong opinions. People who know you best probably have expressed their observation that you indeed relish conflict. The D is about power. Do it because I said so. I am the boss. I am in control. The C is about compliance. Do it because the rules say so. I have the rules in writing. I am the expert in this field. Influenced by the D and C dimensions, you are not easily deterred once you make a decision.

You do experience internal conflict depending on how you view your level of control in relation to your environment. When you feel more powerful, you choose between options quickly often demonstrating extraordinary decisiveness on one hand or uniformed impulse on the other. When you feel less powerful than your environment, you will take time making decisions while deliberating as many considerations and consequences, intended and unintended, as possible. Your desire for rapid success is counterbalanced by an equally strong drive for precision just as your forcefulness is often tempered by your conscientiousness. Perhaps your greatest conflict arises out of your primary need for change and challenge tempered by your secondary inclination towards rules, policies, and security – status quo. As stark as these conflicts appear, you handle them quite smoothly often segueing effortlessly between them as your perceptions of your power changes throughout the day. We will discuss this notion of power and environment in depth later in the text. Please read both the High D (Quadrant 1) and High C (Quadrant 4) narratives in the beginning of this chapter. See if some of the strengths and growth areas of both profiles resonate with you and then consider the applicable suggestions for growth offered in the *Moving Forward* narratives.

The D/I

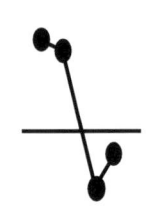

Quadrant 6

The *D/I* profile represents D and I dimensions above the line with S and C below the line. We all are a blend of all four dimensions, but the D/I profile behaves primarily with D tendencies and secondarily with I tendencies. Fluctuating between the two dimensions may appear seamless or abrupt at times. You often act neither as a pure D nor pure I due to the thorough blending of the two dimensions (and the two below the line) creating a profile that is unique in itself. A good example is your ability to flow smoothly between people and things. While you are mission-driven first, you value the journey and the relationships made along the way. You recognize the surest and quickest path to task achievement is through strong leadership founded in credibility and trust with those around you.

Accurate or not, you almost always view yourself as more powerful than your environment. Depending on how you view your circumstances at a specific instance usually will determine your behavior (we will address the notion of power and environment more in Chapter 6). For example, persistence and a competitive spirit define you. You go through life at a face pace looking for new challenges and new opportunities – always willing to stretch routine and accepted boundaries. How you succeed often may fluctuate between behaviors consistent with either the D or I dimension. When you view the environment as unfavorable, the D dimension emergences with power and dominance. When you view your environment as favorable, the I dimension emerges using persuasion, manipulation, and your strong communication skills to succeed.

As with all combinations, sometimes your behavior is the same, but your motive is different. For instance, you occasionally give your office a pretty good cleaning and straightening – nothing too over the top but good. The D in you does it because you cannot seem to get anything accomplished when the cluster gets unruly. The I dimension does it because someone might come in and judge you negatively on the way things look. With D and I above the line, you may fluctuate between both motives or perhaps both motives inform your decision to straighten things.

Appearances matter to you. The D in you works hard, and it is often important to you that others recognize this. You hold yourself to a strong work ethic and you expect no less of those around you regardless of the context. The I in you is creative, moving forward with zeal and enthusiasm. The high I wants recognition for this too – partly because I profiles like the attention but partly because you need to persuade others to your side of whatever the issue is at the time.

With your energy, drive, and impulsive propensities, you want things to happen now. Your sense of urgency is unsurpassed. When things do not happen at the pace you want, you can become annoyed, impatient, and even harsh in word and action. You will attempt to persuade and motivate those around you to get the job done, but your default if that does not work is force and dominance. You are not afraid to make demands of others regardless of their rank or position or their needs. Informed by both the D and I dimensions, you also are quite adept at using words to hurt people. You almost innately sense people's vulnerabilities and have little reservations in exploiting them when you deem necessary.

You can have a great sense of humor but with an edge. Your typical approach at humor is direct and to the point without pulling any punches, and it may include a bit of self-importance. Your picking and poking and having fun at other's expenses if often very funny. However, not knowing where the line is or when to stop can present difficulty for you.

You are confident – sometimes too confident bordering on obnoxious and lacking the ability to recognize your limitations. Your self-assurance manifests not just in the way you carry yourself but, in your motives and actions, as well. Your adventurous spirit needs autonomy. Restrictive environments frustrate and drain you of motivation. No task or goal is ever beyond you. You need the latitude to think big and do big. You love a big stage with big problems and big consequences. As a result, you thrive in challenge and crisis, particularly when all eyes are on you for success. You are a thinker and a doer. Your supervisors, peers, subordinates, family, and friends often look to you to make things happen. Your enthusiasm energizes people, while your dominance can intimidate and alienate at times. You have the uncanny ability to both draw people in and distance them at the same time. Read both the High D (Quadrant 1) and High I (Quadrant 2) narratives in the beginning of this chapter. See if some of the strengths and growth areas of both profiles resonate with you and then consider the applicable suggestions for growth offered in the *Moving Forward* narratives.

The I/D

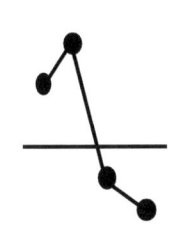

Quadrant 7

The *I/D* profile represents I and D dimensions above the line with S and C below the line. We all are a blend of all four dimensions, but the I/D profile behaves primarily with I tendencies and secondarily with D tendencies. As with D/I profiles, fluctuating between the two dimensions often appears seamless. However, it also can appear sudden. One minute you are playful and the life of the party. The next minute you abruptly tell your spouse it is time to leave. You have probably heard many times in your life, "What just flipped your switch?"

You often act neither as a pure I nor pure D due to the thorough blending of the two dimensions (and the two below the line) creating a profile that is unique in itself. Your primary dimension focuses on people while your secondary focuses on tasks. However, you may bring both dimensions to bear in the same instance. For instance, you are having difficulty getting buy-in from one of your employees on a new priority program. While persuasion is still your tool of choice, you will do it with a sense of urgency, clarity, and force uncommon to those with only the I dimension above the line. Another example is your sense of trust. The I profile is very trusting. The D profile trusts little. The I/D trusts but verifies.

You are adept at using people's intrinsic needs to your advantage. You give friendship to those looking for acceptance. You empower those who need control. You provide security to those who crave status quo. You ask people questions about themselves demonstrating, at least ostensibly, how much you value them. All the while, however, you continue to push and pull throughout the day to bring people to your side, to win them over. Your emotional intelligence is sky high but your commitment to truly caring about people fluctuates depending on all sorts of variables.

As with the D/I profile, you are confident – sometimes too confident biting off more than you can handle. Your self-assurance manifests not just in the way you carry yourself but, in your motives and actions, as well. You value both prestige and power seeking to maintain a position of control throughout the day regardless of the context. You want to be both liked and respected by those around you.

Your ability to captivate an audience, persuade a group of people to your side, or inspire an entire organization or cause, has made you successful time and again. Because of this, you often do not take the appropriate time to plan and prepare. Charisma can be your trap unless you take time to equally build your substance.

Your outgoing tendencies include fun and humor but usually with an edge. Your typical approach at humor is direct and to the point without pulling any punches and may include a bit of self-importance and way for you to take center stage. Your self-deprecating humor, as well as your picking, poking, and having fun at other's expenses, is often very funny. However, not knowing where the line is or when to stop can present difficulty for you.

You need autonomy and challenge – both the I and D dimensions frustrate easily and lose self-motivation in boring and restrictive environments. No task or goal is ever beyond you. You need the latitude to think big and do big. You love a big stage with big problems and big consequences. As a result, you thrive in challenge and crisis, particularly when all eyes are on you for success. Your big-picture view of life is powerfully inspiring. Yet, seeing only the forest filters out the individual trees. This may be a growth area for you regarding people and goals.

You are a thinker and a doer. You are good at selling and closing the deal. Your supervisors, peers, subordinates, family, and friends often look to you to make things happen. While you are people-oriented first, you value the accomplishment of the goal and will resort to force over persuasion if necessary. Your enthusiasm energizes people, but your dominance can intimidate and alienate at times. You are capable of dynamic action or charming affability depending on the needs of the circumstances. You have the uncanny ability to both draw people in and distance them all at the same time. You possess clear goals in life with the resolve and commitment to accomplish them. Please read both the high I (Quadrant 2) and high D (Quadrant 1) narratives in the beginning of this chapter. See if some of the strengths and growth areas of both profiles resonate with you and then consider the applicable suggestions for growth offered in the *Moving Forward* narratives.

The I/S

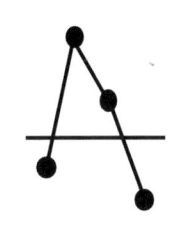

Quadrant 8

The *I/S* profile represents I and S dimensions above the line with D and C below the line. We all are a blend of all four dimensions, but the I/S profile behaves primarily with I tendencies and secondarily with S tendencies. The I/S profile is all about people.

Both the I and S dimensions are more oriented towards feelings and emotions than things. The high S dimension cares about people while the high I dimension has an intellectual and emotional need to understand them. Taken together, the I/S is confident, outgoing, friendly, inquisitive, and empathetic. You are helpful and patient and often willing to compromise as a result. As Will Rogers offered, "Strangers are just people I haven't met yet." You seem to wear a smile on your face more than all other profiles.

You do experience conflict as with the other combination profiles. However, you are very adept at fluctuating between your two high dimensions smoothly and seamlessly to most people. Your orientation towards people over things changes little throughout the day. What does change, however, is your approach – more assertive or more passive, all driven by how you perceive yourself in relation to your environment in that instant – more powerful or less powerful accordingly. The I dimension almost attacks life with risk-taking, vision, and lofty dreams. The S dimension is more reserved, content, and appreciative of security and status quo. Your high I dimension likes to be in charge while your high S dimension is comfortable in supporting roles. You have the capacity to flow between both sides of the same coin almost effortlessly.

Much of the time, you do act quite as an I or quite as an S as the thorough blending together of the two dimensions (and the two below the line) creates a profile that is unique in itself. For instance, you have a colleague who is not quite on board with your vision. You will spend an inordinate amount of time and energy selling your ideas to that person. Your high D colleague would have told him weeks ago to "get on board or jump ship." Your action is consistent with the high I's need to persuade and win others over, but the inordinate amount of time with just one person is much more consistent with the high S dimension. Thus, the I/S profile emerges as a blending of the two.

Charming, sincere, and engaging, you are viewed as the great communicator. Your I dimension is spontaneous and confident allowing you to comfortably speak to the masses while relishing in the spotlight. Your S dimension loves engaging in more trusting and secure smaller groups with friends, family, and coworkers. Regardless of the context, you can be depended upon to carry the conversation.

Because you are so forward-looking and highly oriented towards people, you may often neglect tasks. Regardless of how strong your work ethic, you may find difficulty pulling away from conversations that are draining you of the time needed to complete your tasks. You need human connectivity, and you do not want to hurt other's feelings. You generally do not miss a deadline, but you do not often beat deadlines either.

For the same reasons you sometimes neglect tasks, you also sometimes neglect the facts. You tend to speak in the narrative with more vagueness and generalizations than other profiles. "They've done studies on this." The high C cringes with statements like this. Who are they? What studies? DISC does not measure integrity and character, so don't take offense to this. But you may exaggerate or over generalize from time to time. You sure would not want the facts to get in the way of a good story.

Because the I/S profile is about people, people affect you more than they do other profiles. You constantly are in observation mode scanning people's words, deeds, and non-verbals to gain a nuanced sense of their sincerity and commitment. When life is good with social acceptance and praise, you are energetic, enthusiastic, and happy. However, when you perceive strong confrontation or a loss of social acceptance or friendship, your energy drains, your motivation fades, and your mood turns to sadness and rejection. Just as you are so adept at making people feel good about themselves, you too need to feel that you are appreciated, respected, and liked by the people around you. Please read both the high I (Quadrant 2) and high S (Quadrant 3) narratives in the beginning of this chapter. See if some of the strengths and growth areas of both profiles resonate with you and then consider the applicable suggestions for growth offered in the *Moving Forward* narratives.

The S/I

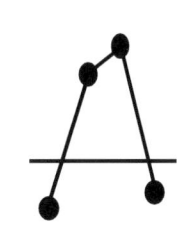

Quadrant 9

The *S/I* profile represents S and I dimensions above the line with D and C below the line. We all are a blend of all four dimensions, but the S/I profile behaves primarily with S tendencies and secondarily with I tendencies. As with your I/S friends, the S/I profile is all about people.

Both the S and I dimensions are more oriented towards feelings and emotions than things. The high S dimension cares about feelings while the high I dimension has an intellectual and emotional need to understand people. Taken together, the S/I profile is thoughtful, welcoming, sympathetic, and inquisitive. You wear a smile on your face with a genuine sense of friendliness and contentment. You likely spend a great deal of your time making new relationships and working on existing ones.

With S as your highest dimension, you are a good listener and not afraid to consider other people's opinions and ideas. You understand the tremendous value in establishing and maintaining trusting relationships. You know the most powerful way to show people you care is to spend time with them. You ask questions demonstrating your concern as well as helping them with problems. The I dimension likes attention for themselves, but you are adept at tempering that pull and letting others have the attention and space. Because of this, people are drawn to you, particularly in times of need. Your easy-going persona presents warmth, comfort, and acceptance. Some days it seems as if you cannot get any work done because people keep talking to you. Everyone wants to tell you their story. Everyone trusts you. Everyone wants to be your friend.

Your soft-spoken friendliness and compassion towards people may be your most endearing qualities. However, when not managed properly, those characteristics can lead to the outright avoidance of conflict and high-pressure situations. They can lead to a lack of assertiveness, clarity in words and tone in tough conversations, and objectivity. Your patience and loyalty, especially with friends, can be a blind spot pushing you to sometimes focus more on the virtues of a person rather than the constructive criticism of their performance.

You do experience conflict as with the other combination profiles. However, you are very adept at fluctuating between your two high dimensions in a seamless fashion. Your orientation towards people over tasks changes little throughout the day. What does change, however, is your approach – more assertive or more passive, all driven by how you perceive yourself in relation to your environment in that instant – more powerful or less powerful accordingly (we will discuss this notion of power and environment in chapter 6). The S dimension is more reserved, satisfied, and appreciative of stability and status quo. The I dimension ambitiously tackles life with grand visions and risk-taking. You have the capacity to flow between both sides of the same coin almost effortlessly.

Because profiles with S and I above the line are about people, people affect them more than they do other profiles. You tend to feel emotional highs and lows more than others. When life is good with social acceptance and appreciation, you are energetic, enthusiastic, and happy. However, when you perceive strong confrontation or a loss of social acceptance or friendship, your energy drains, your motivation fades, and your mood turns to sadness and rejection. You are keenly aware how your words and deeds make others feel and are sensitive enough to alter them when necessary. You project sincerity and sensitivity for others, and you internalize those characteristics just as deeply. Just as you are so adept at making people feel good about themselves, you too need to feel that you are appreciated, respected, and liked by the people around you.

You are great at bringing people together. You know the best way to communicate is to get others to engage with one another. Your listening skills and diplomatic, friendly approach make you the ideal team member. In fact, you are adept at assembling individuals into functioning teams that respect both results and the journey to accomplish them. Please read both the high S (Quadrant 3) and high I (Quadrant 2) narratives in the beginning of this chapter. See if some of the strengths and growth areas of both profiles resonate with you and then consider the applicable suggestions for growth offered in the *Moving Forward* narratives.

The S/C

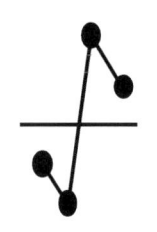

Quadrant 10

The *S/C* profile represents S and C dimensions above the line with I and D below the line. We all are a blend of all four dimensions, but the S/C profile behaves primarily with S tendencies and secondarily with C tendencies. The high S is about people while the high C is about tasks. Taken together, you are a tremendously dependable person who can be counted on to get things done and done right the first time.

Driven by both the S and C dimensions, you approach life at a more patient and slower pace than most other profiles. Because of your even temperament, fair-minded approach, and caring attitude (high S dimension), you need time to consider all sides of issues and ensure everyone's feelings are considered. Your propensity towards accuracy and quality (high C dimension) requires time to plan, prepare, and accomplish your tasks correctly the first time. As a result, time management may be a struggle, particularly with stressful and seemingly overwhelming demands on you. Even if you do not voice it, you resent others for pushing you for quicker results. You move through life best at your own pace free from outside stressors. In fact, your people-orientation can be a stressor. When trying to accomplish something, particularly with a looming deadline, people may represent a huge distraction because you will give them attention instead of working on the task. For the most part, you do not miss deadlines or time tables, but you rarely beat them with a lot of time to spare. You are consistent and stable always with an eye towards quality.

Among your most endearing characteristics, you are sincere, genuine, caring, and loyal. Your humility and deference to others separate you from other profiles. You have no hidden agenda. You are slow to anger. People feel comfortable around you. They trust you. They want to be your friend. They can count on you to maintain composure in stressful situations and offer support and comfort in times of need.

Just as people enjoy your company, you need their company as well. Even with your predisposition for details and facts, you are people-oriented first and foremost. You are sensitive to the needs of others, and you want that same acceptance and support in return. Your feelings may be hurt more easily than other profiles, but the high C in you eventually processes the details of those feelings and surrounding events thus enabling you to move beyond those initial sensitivities. The high C is very capable of holding grudges, especially with people outside of close friends and family, but usually your S dimension prevails with forgiveness and acceptance.

Your high S dimension indicates a need for harmony, security, and stability. Chaos and tense environments are not your friends. Your high C is about compliance with the rules, regulations, and even social expectations. Both dimensions favor status quo and contentment. These inclinations provide a stable and dependable environment for those around you. However, they may lead to a lack of initiative as well as risk aversion, inflexibility, and an overabundance of caution. Unlike your high I and D friends, you live more in the present as opposed to big-picture future initiatives fraught with risk and danger. When you do consider the future, you like it as planned, secured, and settled as much as possible.

You are persistent but may need a little nudging or direction to get started down a particular path. Once you get started, there is no stopping you. However, your persistence, unchecked, may turn to stubbornness. Once your mind is made up, it is very hard to change. You have the capacity to alter your decisions if you deliberately open your mind to new ideas, approaches, and of course, evidence supporting a different path.

You are generally open in your communications and approach with others. You can be quite talkative in small groups of friends and family but often quiet and reserved in large groups, particularly in settings where you do not know people. Your openness also has limitations in situations where you perceive that openness will hurt those around you. It causes you pain to hurt other's feelings, especially those close to you. You are keenly aware how your words and deeds make others feel and are sensitive enough to alter them when necessary.

Your compassion, along with your sense of modesty and need for social acceptance, often manifests in difficulty with conflict. You can be overly reticent to challenge others when you disagree with their position or even when you believe you are being exploited. This may appear to others that you possess a high level of agreeableness. Indeed, much of the time, that would be correct. However, as you well know, people should not assume you agree just because you do not challenge their decisions. A potential growth opportunity may be to work on your ability to confront people in appropriate circumstances. Your natural diplomatic and friendly approach will equip you well. Please read both the high S (Quadrant 3) and high C (Quadrant 4) narratives in the beginning of this chapter. See if some of the strengths and growth areas of both profiles resonate with you and then consider the applicable suggestions for growth offered in the *Moving Forward* narratives.

The C/S

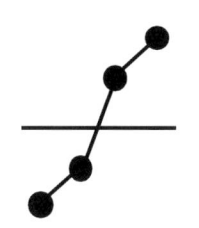

Quadrant 11

The *C/S* profile represents C and S dimensions above the line with I and D below the line. We all are a blend of all four dimensions, but the C/S profile behaves primarily with C tendencies and secondarily with S tendencies. Like your S/C friends and colleagues, you both have S and C dimensions above the line. Thus, you will share many behavioral similarities. But with your C higher than the S, your focus on people will, more often than not, give way to a focus on task and results.

Your high C cares about getting things done and honoring commitments, while your high S cares about people. At your worst, you may be viewed as rigid and caring more about rules, processes, and tasks than the people around you. When you are at your best, perfectly blending the strengths of the C and S dimensions, you are among the most conscientious of all profiles.

While the high C dimension is comfortable *going it alone*, the blending of your C and S results in someone who does find value in being part of the team. You expect clarity, transparency, and clear expectations of individual team members as well as the team as a whole. An ambiguous assembly of people is not a team. As reserved and unemotional as you may seem (sometimes even appearing insensitive), you often want social acceptance and reassurance from those on the team or in your circle of friends and family.

You are a critical thinker strongly valuing precision and facts. You need to understand the way things work at what some would consider a micro level. Indeed, your D and I coworkers may sometimes accuse you of getting too buried in the minutia of a task yet all the while appreciating you are the one who can be counted on to know the rules, focus the team with careful deliberation, and get things done right the first time.

Because of your analytical nature and high value on quality, you place great emphasis on thorough planning and organization, particularly understanding the expectations and requirements of the task. As such, you do not like to be wrong. Even more, you do not like to be told you are wrong. Working towards being less tense and defensive in the face of criticism may be a growth opportunity for you.

You need time to complete your tasks. Short deadlines and last-minute challenges are often strong demotivators for you. You want perfection, and nothing perfect happens without the time to plan and analyze every consideration and consequence. You also are tenacious and resolute but may need a subtle push from time to time to get out of the weeds of a task and see the big picture. Your tenacity may lead to stubbornness making it difficult to change your mind, particularly when your opponent is countering with an emotional argument. Driven by facts and evidence, you need more than eloquent and inspirational verbiage to sway you.

You are normally reserved in your emotions and communications often letting the facts speak for themselves. In fact, it is within your comfort zone to spend much of your time alone even to the point of becoming isolated from others. You do enjoy the company of a coworker, friend, or family member but not so much for idle chat. Your favorite conversations often center around the details of an issue and offer a platform where you can share your knowledge or learn something new from the other person. While you dislike conflict and are usually diplomatic in your communications, you can become irritated, even contentious, when what you perceive as unrealistic expectations and time restraints are thrust upon you. You do not like uncertainty. You frustrate more easily than most profiles when those around you ignore the rules or make up their own. Because of your self-control and discipline, it disturbs you when others fail to plan appropriately. High I profiles who like to *wing it* (and often succeed in this way) simply leave you speechless.

Your high C is about compliance with rules, protocols, and even societal expectations. Your high S indicates harmony, security, and stability. Confusion, disorder, and stressful environments are not your friends. Both dimensions favor status quo and contentment. These dispositions provide a stable, reliable, and dependable environment for those around you. However, these qualities may lead to a lack of creativity and decisiveness as well as rigidity, aversion to risk, and an overabundance of caution. Yet, in times of stress, the C/S profile (particularly if the D dimension is just below line) may make decisions very quickly and efficiently.

Unlike the high I and D profiles, you prefer the safety and predictability of status quo as opposed to risky endeavors fraught with spontaneity, uncertainty, and peril. When you do consider the untested and unknown, you like to contemplate, to the extent possible, every conceivable scenario and potential outcome. Humble and impartial, you are always prepared, diligent, and hardworking, and will never willingly let those close to you down. Please read both the high C (Quadrant 4) and high S (Quadrant 3) narratives in the beginning of this chapter. See if some of the strengths and growth areas of both profiles resonate with you and then consider the applicable suggestions for growth offered in the *Moving Forward* narratives.

The C/D

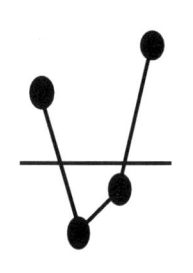

Quadrant 12

The *C/D* profile represents C and D dimensions above the line with I and S below the line. We all are a blend of all four dimensions, but the C/D profile behaves primarily with C tendencies and secondarily with D tendencies. You are persistent and results-driven. The C in you is about perfection, accuracy, and intellectual curiosity. The D is active, almost zealous in your approach to life. You may be best characterized as someone who wants things done right and done in the manner of your choosing.

You are self-disciplined, deliberate, and focused. You can block out distractions better than most people. When immersed in a project, you may not even hear those around you talking or the TV or the phone ring or even a siren outside. You are a hard worker. You are no quitter. In fact, you can be absolutely dogged in your quest to learn, build, and lead.

Often the loner, you seldom seek advice from other people. When you do, you ask sharp questions even if unpopular. You prefer to learn and create through trial and error, or you study alone. You will work with others, particularly as you have matured over the years, but you still would rather work alone or with a close friend or associate you trust who will not consume your day with idle chat. You frustrate easily when you must wait for others to do their part, and frankly, you do not like to share control. You are highly critical of both yourself and others with a tendency to correct people when they make mistakes, even to the point of highlighting errors they may view as minor and inconsequential.

You do not relish confrontation, but you do not shrink from it. You are strong in your convictions and not afraid to let people know. Indeed, you often can be counted on to express contrary views, play the role of devil's advocate, helping those around you see all sides of an issue. Your bluntness is sometimes perceived as fresh and honest with no hidden agenda. Yet, sometimes it is perceived as cold, insensitive, condescending, and even sanctimonious. You can be skeptical of people's motives and sometimes prefer not to share information unless necessary. When communication with others is essential, you tend to be clear and concise, focusing on practical issues and tasks. Small talk with no defined end does not sit well with you.

You recognize not enough time exists in the day for you to get everything you want to be accomplished done alone. You know delegation is the only path, and you can be very adept at providing direction and orders. Yet, your propensity to *go it alone* can get in the way. When you delegate, you can be clear in your communication and precise with the instructions. Yet, you also can micromanage and become very critical when things do not progress in the time or way you deem appropriate. You believe in getting things done right and rarely are afraid to offer your position forcefully and directly.

Willpower abounds in your approach to tasks. You are intensely persistent and have strong opinions. The C is about compliance. Do it because the rules say so. I have the rules in writing. I am the expert in this field. The D is about power. Do it because I said so. I am the boss. I am in charge. Influenced by both dimensions, you are not easily deterred once you make a decision, and you rarely ever quit something once you start. Failure and lack of control are your greatest nemeses. Your tenacity may lead to stubbornness making it difficult to change your mind, particularly when your opponent is countering with an emotional argument. Driven by facts and evidence, you need more than eloquent and inspirational verbiage to sway you.

You do experience internal conflict depending on how you view your level of control in relation to your environment. When you feel less powerful than your environment (C dimension), you will take time making decisions while deliberating as many considerations and consequences as possible. When you feel more powerful (D dimension), you choose between options quickly often demonstrating extraordinary decisiveness on one hand or uniformed impulse on the other. Your desire for precision and quality is counterbalanced by an equally strong drive to accomplish things quickly just as your conscientiousness is tempered by your assertive nature. Perhaps your greatest conflict arises out of your primary need for compliance (rules, policies, security) challenged by your secondary need for change, risk, and uncertainty. As stark as these conflicts appear, you handle them smoothly often segueing effortlessly between them as your perceptions of your power changes throughout the day. We will discuss this notion of power and environment in depth later in the text. Please read both the High C (Quadrant 4) and High D (Quadrant 1) narratives in the beginning of this chapter. See if some of the strengths and growth areas of both profiles resonate with you and then consider the applicable suggestions for growth offered in the *Moving Forward* narratives.

The D/S

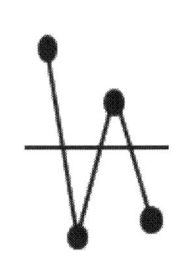

Quadrant 13

The *D/S* profile represents D and S dimensions above the line with I and C below the line. We all are a blend of all four dimensions, but the D/S profile behaves primarily with D tendencies and secondarily with S tendencies. This profile is so rare, many instruments do not even address it. It is estimated that only ½ of 1% of the population has the D/S or S/D profile.

You often act neither as a pure D nor pure S due to the thorough blending of the two dimensions (and the two below the line) creating a profile that is unique in itself. Your primary dimension focuses on task while your secondary focuses on people. However, you may bring both dimensions to bear in the same instance. For instance, one of your employees betrays your trust. Your high D values results while your high S values loyalty. This blend of the two manifests when you hold the employee accountable for his behavior while still affording him a second chance.

You are a doer. The high D is laser-focused on results. The high S brings the "worker bee" ethic to the mix. Your high D is independent in nature leading you to trust your abilities and judgment more than those of your colleagues. Your friendly and caring high S does not like to impose on others. As a result, delegation may be difficult for you even when appropriate. However, a savvy D/S has learned through trial and error that very little in life gets accomplished without relying on self and others.

You also tend to be realistic and objective in your approach. You like to have your own space to deal with problems and tasks – a space where you can set your own timelines, pace, and approach to the extent possible. As strong as the high D can be, you still lack self-confidence on occasion. As a result, you may be a little slow to start new things, but once you do, you almost never turn back. You are genuine and transparent. The D values straightforward communication, and the S values transparency and relationships. You are equally known for your determination and willpower as well as your lack of a hidden agenda. People appreciate and respect those characteristics in you.

You generally do not like to get wrapped up in details. If necessary, you can force yourself into the weeds of an issue, but details and minutiae frustrate you. There is the goal. Let's go make it happen. Details and preparation are obstacles to only slow you down. Similarly, you appreciate structure and routine, but you easily become demoralized in a restrictive environment where you do not have a sense of control. Control to you does not mean barking out orders although commanding others to do your bidding is well within your comfort zone. Control to you may mean sitting back and watching quietly knowing you are in control or contemplating ways to gain control should the need arise.

You can be very stubborn and opinionated, and you definitely have an independent streak. Holding your ground once a decision is made gives you the appearance of strength and conviction. However, overused this characteristic can lead others to see rigidity and self-righteousness. Sometimes you do enjoy a good intellectual fight, but more often than not, you will not change your mind in the end based on emotional arguments. For someone to win an argument with you, she will need crystal clear logic or factual evidence. Even then, you almost need to tangibly feel a lesson to learn from it. You listen to people and appear to value their interest and advice, but you go through life with trial and error as your guide. Sometimes it takes two or three failures using the same behavior in the same context for you to alter your course.

You clearly experience internal conflict, perhaps more than any other profile. You experience conflict with both how you perceive your environment (favorable or unfavorable) and how you perceive your power in relation to that environment (more powerful or less powerful). We will explore this notion of control and environment further in chapter 6. The high D is about power and control, more about results than people. The high S is about warmth and teamwork, more about people than results. Fluctuating between the two dimensions may appear smooth and seamless, or it may appear quite abrupt at times. You may be yelling one minute and apologizing the next. You also segue throughout the day from feeling more powerful than your circumstances to feeling less powerful. You can be the domineering leader in one context and the submissive follower in the next. This explains how in one moment you are barking orders in full command while in another moment sitting in the back of the room shy and reserved. A D/S friend of mine was a dominant, risk-taking, powerhouse within the walls of the business he owned. Yet, when out in public (stores, restaurants), he was cautious, subdued, even a little timid. The stark change in his behavior was so bizarre to me until I learned the DISC model.

As you mature and learn to flow smoothly between the conflicting D and S dimensions, you display strength, confidence, and power balanced with fairness, loyalty, and support for those around you. Your capacity to value both results and compassion serves you well in leadership positions - supporting your people but also holding them accountable. *Tough love* may well define your approach. Read both the high D (Quadrant 1) and high S (Quadrant 3) narratives in the beginning of this chapter. See if some of the strengths and growth areas of both profiles resonate with you and then consider the applicable suggestions for growth offered in the *Moving Forward* narratives.

The I/C

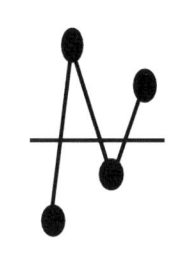

Quadrant 14

The *I/C* profile represents I and C dimensions above the line with D and S below the line. We all are a blend of all four dimensions, but the I/C profile behaves primarily with I tendencies and secondarily with C tendencies. This profile is rare. Indeed, many instruments do not even address it. It is estimated that only 3% of the population have the I/C or C/I profile.

DISC is predicated on perception – how you perceive your environment (favorable or unfavorable) and how you perceive yourself in relation to that environment (less powerful or more powerful). We will talk much more about this dynamic later in the text. Your I dimension emerges when you perceive your environment as favorable. When you are happy and want to be where you are doing what you want, you are friendly and outgoing. When you perceive your environment as unfavorable (for whatever reason), your C dimension tends to take over. You become withdrawn, impatient, even critical and will focus on task over people.

You like to blend your creative ideas with pragmatism and purpose. You can be very direct but generally avoid harsh dialogue because you care about other's feelings although this can change in stressful or unfavorable environments. Your preferred style of motivation is persuasion, explaining the reasons behind the action, and leading by example in word and deed.

You clearly experience internal conflict, much more than most other profiles. While your primary dimension focuses on people, you may shift quickly to a focus on task and results. Your high I dimension is all about people, impulsiveness, risk, and the future. Your high C is about things, certainty, compliance, and status quo. You sometimes cannot see the trees for forest, and other times cannot see the forest for the trees. You can be a risk-taker, or someone trapped in caution. You can be unplanned preferring to *wing it*, or you may be strongly organized and almost overly prepared. You may be the life of the party one minute and wanting nothing to do with people the next. You may be a big-picture dreamer in one setting and married to rules and policies in another. Fluctuating between these two conflicting dimensions may appear smooth and seamless, or it may appear quite abrupt at times.

You often act neither as a pure I nor pure C due to the thorough blending of the two dimensions (and the two below the line) creating a profile that is unique in itself. Your primary dimension focuses on people while your secondary focuses on tasks. However, you may bring both dimensions to bear in the same instance. Perhaps the simplest way this blending of the two dimensions manifests is with your conversations. You enjoy engaging with people but want the conversation to have substance and value where you both grow from it. In fact, sometimes you can lose track of time in a discussion unaware that the other person would like to bring it to a conclusion. You also tend to think out loud because you value the dynamic of working through challenges with others. While collaboration can be powerful, it can lead to long debates that go in circles seemingly never arriving at a clear conclusion.

Consider another example concerning a professor I worked with for many years. He loved the stage. The more people in the audience, the better. He not only was a great presenter in these large groups but also had the ability to work the audience with what appeared to be a natural flow spinning easily from one audience member's comments to the next. What only a few of us knew was that public speaking terrified him. To mitigate his fears, he planned and prepared more than anyone I ever knew. He even prepared specific phrases just in case an audience member asked a very specific question in a very specific manner. And not only would he study and prepare, he would also practice saying certain things in different ways in the mirror.

You can begin to see how conflicted the I/C profile can be, but also how beautifully the savvy I/C can blend those two dimensions into a single, extremely effective profile.

As you mature and learn to flow smoothly between the conflicting I and C dimensions, you display confidence and charisma balanced with fairness and critical thinking. You tend to be a strong communicator – your high C choosing your words prudently and your high I naturally gifted at influencing others. Your capacity to value both compassion and results serves you well in leadership positions - supporting your people but also holding them accountable. Please read both the high I (Quadrant 2) and high C (Quadrant 4) narratives in the beginning of this chapter. See if some of the strengths and growth areas of both profiles resonate with you and then consider the applicable suggestions for growth offered in the *Moving Forward* narratives.

The S/D

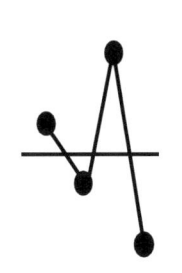

Quadrant 15

The *S/D* profile represents S and D dimensions above the line with I and C below the line. We all are a blend of all four dimensions, but the S/D profile behaves primarily with S tendencies and secondarily with D tendencies. This profile is so rare, many instruments do not even address it. It is estimated that only ½ of 1% of the population have the D/S or S/D profile.

Your primary dimension focuses on people while your secondary focuses on tasks. Taken together, you tend to be realistic and objective in your outlook but also conscientious in your approach. You place a high value on productivity. You may even judge yourself (and others) at the end of the day based on how much you accomplished. You also value how you accomplish the goal. You try hard to be considerate of others and not hurt feelings, but in stressful times, you will resort to a more authoritative and domineering approach. Because you are people-oriented, you are inclined to take time for people even when you do not have that time to give. As a result, particularly with pressing deadlines and unfinished work, people can actually frustrate you when you perceive their presence as an obstacle to accomplishing your set goal.

You enjoy tough challenges but like to have your own space to deal with them – a space where you set your own timelines, pace, and approach to the extent possible. You do not respond well to others looking over your shoulders, hurrying you, and setting what you perceive as unrealistic time frames. You listen to people and sincerely value their interest and advice, but you tend to go through life with trial and error as your guide. Sometimes it takes two or three failures using the same behavior in the same context for you to alter your course. Your high S values transparency and relationships while your D values straightforward communication. People respect your fairness and sincerity as well as your strong determination and willpower.

Even with D as your secondary dimension, you still can lack self-confidence from time to time. Coupled with a strong sense of consciousness, often you will not delegate responsibilities because you do not want to overburden those around you, or you simply know things will get done if you do it yourself. From time to time, you may be a little slow to get out of your comfort zone and start new things, but once you do, you never turn back. You are determined, persistent, and unflappable. Savvy S/Ds are very adept at giving others credit for a job well done while taking the blame when things do not go well.

Although you are adept at problem-solving and critical thinking, you rarely like to get wrapped up in details. If necessary, you can force yourself into the weeds of an issue, but details and minutiae frustrate you. You sometimes view specifics and preparation as obstacles that only slow you down from your goals. You appreciate structure and routine, but you easily become demoralized in a restrictive environment where you do not have a sense of control.

You experience internal conflict more than most profiles. Your high D is about power and control, more about results than people. Your high S is about warmth and teamwork, more about people than results. Your high S is patient, while your high D is impulsive. Your high S wants peace and harmony, while your high D thrives in conflict and confrontation. Fluctuating between the two dimensions may appear smooth and seamless, or it may appear quite abrupt at times. You may be yelling one minute and apologizing the next. You can be the domineering leader in one context and the consummate follower in the next. One moment you are sitting in the back of the room somewhat shy and reserved and in the next moment barking orders in full command of the situation.

As you mature and learn to flow smoothly between the conflicting S and D dimensions, you display fairness, loyalty, and sincerity for those around you balanced with strength, confidence, and power. Your capacity to value both compassion and results serves you well in leadership positions - supporting your people but also holding them accountable. Please read both the high S (Quadrant 3) and high D (Quadrant 1) narratives in the beginning of this chapter. See if some of the strengths and growth areas of both profiles resonate with you and then consider the applicable suggestions for growth offered in the *Moving Forward* narratives.

The C/I

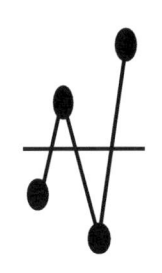

Quadrant 16

The *C/I* profile represents C and I dimensions above the line with D and S below the line. We all are a blend of all four dimensions, but the I/C profile behaves primarily with I tendencies and secondarily with C tendencies. This profile is rare. Indeed, many instruments do not even address it. It is estimated that only 3% of the population have the I/C or C/I profile.

DISC is predicated on perception – how you perceive your environment (favorable or unfavorable) and how you perceive yourself in relation to that environment (less powerful or more powerful). We will talk much more about this dynamic later in the text. Your C dimension emerges when you perceive your environment as unfavorable. You become withdrawn, impatient, even critical and will focus on task over people. When you perceive your environment as favorable, your I dimension tends to take over. When you are happy and want to be where you are doing what you want, you are friendly, outgoing, even charismatic rallying people to your cause.

You often act neither as a pure C nor pure I due to the thorough blending of the two dimensions (and the two below the line) creating a profile that is unique in itself. Your primary dimension focuses on task while your secondary focuses on people. However, you may bring both dimensions to bear in the same instance. For instance, you like to blend creativity (high I dimension) with pragmatism (high C dimension). You are adept at combining intuition, logic, and critical thinking with strong people skills. Your preferred tools of motivation represent a blend of both dimensions as well - persuading, explaining the reasons behind the decision or task, and leading by example in word and deed. Perhaps the simplest way the blending of the two dimensions manifests is with your conversations. You can very direct but generally avoid harsh dialogue because you care about other's feelings although this can change in stressful or unfavorable environments. You enjoy engaging with people but want the conversation to have substance and value where you both grow from it. In fact, sometimes you can lose track of time in a discussion unaware that the other person would like to bring it to a conclusion. While collaboration can be powerful, it can lead to long debates that go in circles seemingly never arriving at a clear conclusion.

You may be hypersensitive to scrutiny because of the extraordinary effort and precision you put into everything you do coupled with your need (even if not self-evident) for social approval. You believe accuracy and details matter, but you also value the needs and feelings of those around you. At your worst, you may be viewed as self-righteous and self-absorbed. At your best, you have the capacity to be a person of significant power and influence.

You experience internal conflict more than most other profiles. While your primary dimension focuses on results, you may shift quickly to a focus on people. Your high C is about tasks, caution, compliance, and status quo. Your high I dimension is about people, impulsiveness, risk, and the future. Your perception of environment and self also affects your external lens. You sometimes cannot see the trees for forest, and other times cannot see the forest for the trees. You can be buried in caution and over-analysis or adept at risk-taking and spontaneity. You can be strongly deliberate and organized or unplanned and unprepared preferring to *wing it* with your charm and gift of gab. You may be the life of the party one minute and wanting nothing to do with people the next. You may be married to rules and policies in one setting and a big-picture dreamer in another. Fluctuating between these two conflicting dimensions may appear smooth and seamless, or it may appear quite abrupt at times.

PAGE | 44

As you mature and learn to flow smoothly between the conflicting I and C dimensions, you display fairness and critical thinking balanced with confidence and optimism. You display strong communication skills – your high I dimension naturally gifted at influencing others and your high C dimension choosing your words prudently. Your capacity to value both results and compassion serves you well in leadership positions - supporting your people but also holding them accountable. Please read both the high C (Quadrant 4) and high I (Quadrant 2) narratives in the beginning of this chapter. See if some of the strengths and growth areas of both profiles resonate with you and then consider the applicable suggestions for growth offered in the *Moving Forward* narratives.

The Tight Profile

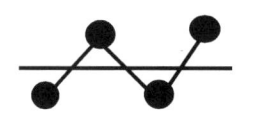

Quadrant 17

The *Tight* profile (sometimes referred to as a flat, neutral, or compressed pattern) represents all four dimensions very close to the horizontal line. It indicates you value all four dimensions with relatively equal importance probably contradicting one another at times with your responses on the assessment. Because of this dynamic and that this profile is very rare (some estimates are as low as 1% of the population), I recommend taking the assessment again with a clearer focus, a clearer context in mind. Also, ask yourself if you feel you were over-analyzing the questions in the assessment by taking too long to respond? Finally, ask yourself if you really understood the meaning of each of the words and the correct process to complete the assessment. The reason I offer these suggestions is the tight profile indicates self-contradictory responses, so much so they combine to cancel each other out resulting in this pattern.

If the pattern remains unchanged after retaking the assessment, it may indicate stress or discomfort in your life such as a significant emotional event, personal trauma, or unusually stressful external environment. More likely, the tight pattern probably indicates a profile devoid of extremes. You do not enjoy the strengths of the four dimensions to the extent as do other profiles, but you do not suffer the growth areas found in all four dimensions to the same extent either. For the most part, you are even-tempered, steady, and adaptable to most situations. Yet, your behavior may still strongly represent any of the four dimensions completely based on your perceptions.

More than any other profile, you flow between all four dimensions equally throughout the day depending on how you view your setting and yourself in relation to that setting. When you view your environment as unfavorable and yourself as more powerful, you behave in a manner consistent with the high D dimension – power, control, and confidence. When you view your environment as favorable and yourself as more powerful, you behave in the high I dimensions – outgoing, talkative, and persuasive. When you view your environment as favorable and yourself as less powerful than the environment, you behave in the S dimensions – sincere, supportive, and steady. When you view your environment as unfavorable and yourself as less powerful, you behave in the C dimension – cautious, compliant, and critical.

Please read all four narratives (D, I, S, and C) in the beginning of this chapter. I imagine you will find parts of you in all four. Do what you can to pull from the applicable strengths and weaknesses of all four profiles and consider the applicable suggestions for growth offered in the *Moving Forward* narratives.

Made in the USA
Middletown, DE
16 September 2025